BARBARA A. SLAUGHTER

I Have a Project of My Own, So I Need to Say No to You, You, and You

I Have a Project of My Own, So I Need to Say No to You, You, and You
Copyright © 2025 by Barbara A. Slaughter

ISBN: 979-8894792132 (hc)
ISBN: 979-8894792118 (sc)
ISBN: 979-8894792125 (e)

The Reading Glass Books
1-888-420-3050
www.readingglassbooks.com
fulfillment@readingglassbooks.com

To my children, grandchildren, and great-grandchildren,
I love you so much!

Acknowledgment

First and foremost, I give GOD all the glory and honor for helping me through all these years. I wrote my first poem between the ages of twelve and sixteen, and it has been a journey of faith, healing, and purpose ever since.

Thank you to the consultant, publisher, and the entire team who supported this project. To Apostle Michelle Cooper, my dear friend and spiritual daughter, thank you for giving me the push I needed to finally birth this vision. To my granddaughter Talisha, and to my friend and neighbor Delilah, your encouragement and presence have meant so much.

Contents

CHAPTER 1

Time Management

Time management refers to the deliberate planning and regulation of how one allocates time to tasks and responsibilities. Effective time management enhances productivity, reduces stress, improves work quality, and creates space for creative pursuits.

Tips for Improving Time Management:

1. Set clear goals: Define what you want to achieve and break it into manageable steps.

2. Avoid overcommitment: Learn to recognize your limits and say no when necessary.

3. Apply the 4 Ds: Do tasks immediately, Defer those that can wait, Delegate when possible, and Delete unnecessary tasks.

4. Enhance information processing: Organize your thoughts and materials to reduce decision fatigue.

5. Cultivate good habits: Establish routines that support focus and efficiency.

Ask yourself: How do I truly spend my time each day? Are my actions aligned with my goals and values?

I've never liked wasting time, yet I must admit, I've spent far too long sitting on this project. Instead of focusing on my own goals, I've often prioritized helping others. Many women do this; we tend to put everyone else's needs before our own. Is it because we are natural nurturers? We offer food, protection, support, encouragement, and guidance. Or perhaps we simply struggle to say no. I learned this lesson the hard way after entrusting my original poems to someone who promised to help publish them. That experience taught me a valuable lesson about boundaries and self-prioritization.

Let me take you back to where it all began. This is the story of a twelve-year-old girl named Barbara Ann Cabell, born on February 23, 1957, in Woodmere, New York. She lived on Lawrence Avenue in Long Island and attended PS #1. Her mother, Marlene Denise Cabell, was a single parent.

My story begins with a young girl named Barbara—me. Life was challenging from the start. I often didn't know where my next meal would come from because my mother was frequently absent. I'd eat with the Jones family or buy a TV dinner from Johnny's grocery store downstairs, charging it to our tab.

I still remember the taste of welfare cheese and peanut butter—oddly delicious, and a comfort I still enjoy today. During those early years, Marlene had the opportunity to assist Delegate James Deleston and Congresswoman Shirley Chisholm.

We lived in a two-bedroom apartment and shared a kitchen with a neighbor. I can still picture that place vividly as I write—every corner etched into memory.

My best friend growing up was Linda Richie. We went to the same beautician and always got our hair done together. Linda had long, beautiful black hair that she wore in two braids down her back—a style I admired and remember vividly.

I often traveled to Far Rockaway, New York, and later discovered that my sister Janice lived there. I also visited Hempstead, where my father, aunts, and cousins resided. These places held pieces of my identity, scattered across the map like breadcrumbs leading back to family.

As the song says, *"You don't know my story, you don't know the things I've been through."* Just wait a while—there's more to tell.

In the summer of 1969, I was away at camp, enjoying a day on the river in a small boat. I had lost my glasses and wasn't feeling well, but I didn't think much of it—until a counselor began waving frantically, calling us back to shore.

There had been an emergency. My mother had passed away.

I packed my things in a daze and was taken to the airport. I boarded the plane alone, unsure of what awaited me. When I landed, a woman met me and gently explained that I would be going to a foster home. Soon after, I was introduced to a lady and a teenage girl. I was told I would be living with them for a while.

By August of that same year, I arrived in Lynchburg, Virginia. I was placed in the home of Mr. and Mrs. Joseph and Mabel Oliver, along with their daughter, Janice.

I had always dreamed of having an older sister—and now, I did. Later, I was introduced to their son, William (Billy). Janice Cheryl helped Ma Mabel with cooking and cleaning inside the house, while I took on the outdoor chores. I grew to love feeding the chickens, cows, and pigs, tending to the vegetable and flower gardens, and stacking wood on the back porch.

Ma Mabel's roses were breathtaking—vibrant and full of life. Neighbors would often stop by just to admire them. Despite all I learned, I never quite mastered the art of milking a cow.

Billy had his own family who lived in the Bronx, New York. They visited occasionally, bringing a sense of connection to the wider world beyond Lynchburg.

Ma Mabel worked at Randolph-Macon Women's College, where she cleaned the chapel. I remember helping her once; it felt special to be part of her routine. Daddy Joe worked for Esteppe Oldsmobile, delivering and picking up car parts, and also held jobs in two of the college's kitchens. He drove an olive green Oldsmobile and a double-cab blue truck—vehicles I came to recognize as symbols of his hard work.

The property's grounds were beautiful, filled with crepe myrtle trees and hydrangea bushes. I was fascinated to learn that pouring dishwater on the hydrangeas could change their color. Everything about this place was new to me—strange, wonderful, and full of discovery.

We lived between two homes—a three-bedroom house and a two-bedroom trailer. During the spring and summer, we stayed in the trailer, and in the fall and winter, we moved into the house.

I attended Boonsboro Elementary and entered the sixth grade. I even had a crush on one of my teachers. Sometimes I walked to school alone—it wasn't far, just down Boonsboro Road. Our neighborhood included five families along Old Boonsboro Road, which is now called Raiford Circle.

There were good days and bad ones. Eventually, the Olivers adopted me, just as they had adopted Janice and Billy. It was a big adjustment. I had to get used to saying "yes, ma'am" and "no, ma'am," a formality that felt foreign to me. I remember thinking, *What is this place? Am I in Never Land?*

School had just been integrated, and the transition was painful. Many of the Black students didn't want to be my friend. I was told, *"You're not in Long Island anymore. Forget those friends."* The letters I wrote probably never got mailed. I was even told, *"You're never going to be anything."* Those words cut deep, but they didn't define me.

One day, overwhelmed and desperate, I ran away with a girl I rode the bus with—she lived in the mountains. I only stayed a few hours before asking her family to take me back home. I begged them to stay a while so I wouldn't get in trouble. I was scared, but thankfully, I wasn't punished.

The house we lived in didn't have running water or a bathroom for a time. The kitchen had both a wood cook stove and an electric one. The front porch was screened in, and I was told the house had once been a store before it caught fire and was renovated.

We weren't allowed to go many places, but I did get to attend my prom—thanks to my sister and cousin, who waited outside for me. It felt like a Cinderella moment. And while it wasn't perfect, it was better than not going at all. *Right? Right.*

As the years passed, tragedy struck again. My Aunt Frances, who lived down the road, had a fire at her house. She made it out safely at first, but went back inside, and tragically, she didn't make it out the second time.

In 1975, Ma Mabel became ill and was admitted to the hospital. She was diagnosed with a brain tumor. Sadly, she passed away before she could see me graduate that June. I had now lost both of my mothers.

After her passing, everything began to unravel. Daddy Joe started drinking heavily and became increasingly volatile. We fought often, and eventually, Janice and I had to stay at our cousin's house down the road. But even there, we weren't safe; Daddy Joe showed up, threatening our cousin, who had no one to protect her after her husband passed away.

His friends would mock me relentlessly. I often hid outside for hours whenever company came over, trying to disappear. It was during this time—when I felt most invisible and unheard—that I began to write poems. Writing became my refuge, my voice, and my way of surviving the chaos.

Psalm 23:1–6: *"The Lord is my shepherd: I shall not want. He maketh me lie down in green pastures: He leadeth me beside still waters. He restoreth my soul: he leadeth me in the path of righteousness for his name's sake. Yea, though I walk through the valley of the shadow of death, I will fear no evil: for thou art with me; thy rod and thy staff they comfort me. Thou preparest a table before me in the presence of my enemies: thou anointest my head with oil: my cup runneth over. Surely goodness and mercy shall follow me all the days of my life: and I will dwell in the house of the Lord forever. "*

Eventually, Janice and I moved into an apartment in Madison Heights. I enrolled at Central Virginia Community College (CVCC), hoping to take a step forward in my education. But it didn't last—I ended up leaving before completing my studies.

Time passed, and I stayed with a friend while Janice returned home. Then, in a moment of divine intervention, things began to shift. Daddy Joe went to a camp in Covington, and Janice and I secured our first jobs at the Williams Home. We truly enjoyed working there; it gave us a sense of independence and purpose.

At the Williams Home, Janice and I worked serving meals and drinks to the ladies; someone else handled the cooking. One of our cousins worked there too, along with a woman who lived on Bedford Avenue. Our shift ran from 5:00 to 7:30 p.m., and it felt empowering to earn our own money. It gave us a break from the chaos at home and a chance to contribute to household expenses.

With our earnings, we could finally go shopping for ourselves, catch a movie, or enjoy a meal out. Thank God, we were free! We'd visit Colemans to buy shoes, and I remember being amazed at how many pairs I owned. We also shopped at Hills and other stores, picking out matching outfits in different colors for the weekend. It felt incredible to buy my own clothes. I was just 99 pounds, yet somehow wearing sizes 16 and 18—something I laugh about now, but it was all part of the journey.

I believe Janice was attending Lynchburg College when I came on the scene. We spent a lot of time on Taylor Street. Janice and Betty would study together, while I babysat two children, ages seven and eleven. We often went to the playground at Robert S. Payne School, visited friends, and occasionally treated ourselves to Dairy Queen. Those moments gave us a sense of normalcy and joy.

At sixteen, I was baptized at Holcomb Rock Baptist Church by Reverend N.S. Walker, a milestone in my spiritual journey. As time went on, Daddy Joe passed away. Despite everything, I forgave him, and he asked for my forgiveness, too. It was one of the hardest things I've ever done.

Colossians 3:13: *"As the Lord has forgiven you, so must you also forgive."*

Ephesians 4:31–32: *"Let all bitterness and wrath and anger and clamor and slander be put away from you, with all malice. Be kind to one another, tenderhearted, forgiving one another, as God in Christ forgave you."*

I met David Slaughter, and we were married on July 16, 1997. Our ceremony took place at the pastor's house, followed by a small reception with family and friends. At the time, Daddy Joe wasn't in attendance.

He had been struggling emotionally, even showing hostility when his sister came to visit. Eventually, they reconciled and forgave one another, a healing moment for our family. Later, we renewed our marriage vows at Mt. Shiloh in Monroe, and this time, Daddy Joe walked me down the aisle. Family and friends were present, and it was a meaningful celebration. We renewed our vows a third time at the Church of God of Prophecy, and each ceremony was beautiful in its own way. David and I were blessed with three children.

In 1992, I faced a serious legal charge that required counseling and court costs. It was one of the most painful experiences of my life. I fell into a deep depression—but through it all, my family stood by me. Their support helped me begin the long journey toward healing.

Through that darkness, I clung to my faith. *My God is awesome.*

Psalm 95:3–5: *"The Lord is a great God and a great King above all gods. In his hand are the deep places of the earth: the strength of the hills is his also. The sea is his, and he made it: and his hands formed the dry land."*

God is great—loving, compassionate, forgiving, and mighty.

Thank you, Jesus!

Time is precious. Don't waste it.

CHAPTER 2

From Darkness to Marvelous Light

Habakkuk 2:2–3: *"And the Lord Answered Me, And Said, Write the Vision, And Make It Plain Upon Tables, That He May Run That Readeth It. For The Vision Is Yet for an Appointed Time, But At the end it shall speak, and not lie, though it tarry, wait for it, because it will surely come, it will not tarry. I just can't thank God enough so filled up right now."*

Jeremiah 1:5: *"Before I formed thee in the belly I knew thee, and before thou comest forth out of thee I sanctified thee, and I ordained thee the prophet unto the nation."*

Jeremiah 29:11: *"For I know the plans I have, for you declares the Lord, thoughts of peace and not of evil, to give you and expected end."*

This is more than a dream come true.

What are we sitting on, family? Friends, sisters, brothers, believers—do you realize the power within you?

What a wonderful God He is! He brought me out of darkness into His marvelous light. *What a wonderful God He is!*

Wow. Wow. Wow.

I know my identity. My name is Victory. Victory—that's my name.

CHAPTER 3

Procrastination

Procrastination means to delay or postpone something. It's often described as being slow or late in doing tasks that should be completed, sometimes due to avoidance, lack of motivation, or even laziness.

Did you know there are four types of procrastinators?

1. **The Performer** – waits until the last minute to feel pressure.

2. **The Self-Deprecator** – feels lazy or inadequate.

3. **The Overbooker** – uses busyness as a shield.

4. **The Novelty Seeker** – constantly starts new things but rarely finishes.

Procrastination can be linked to deeper issues such as depression, anxiety, low self-esteem, ADHD, and poor study habits.

The Bible speaks clearly about procrastination:

- *"Yea, if thou criest after knowledge, and liftest up thy voice for understanding."* —*Proverbs 2:3*

- *"The soul of the sluggard desireth, and hath nothing: but the soul of the diligent shall be made fat."* —Proverbs 13:4

- *"The way of the slothful man is as a hedge of thorns: but the way of the righteous is made plain."* —Proverbs 15:19

- *"He also that is slothful in his work is brother to him that is a great waster."* —Proverbs 18:9

Procrastination can even become a spiritual issue when we delay giving our time, resources, or ourselves to God. Both the lazy and the procrastinator often struggle with motivation.

I've also wondered: where do hoarders come from? It turns out hoarding is often a mental health condition triggered by trauma. It can involve cognitive challenges such as indecisiveness and perfectionism.

In 1993, we moved to the Hopewell–Petersburg area. By then, Daddy Joe had already passed away. The town reminded me of Lynchburg—small, familiar, and quiet. David's brother and his wife were a great help to us during that time.

When we arrived, the place we moved into hadn't even been cleaned. The glass in the back door was shattered, and we had a lot of work ahead of us just to make it livable. David found jobs at a couple of restaurants, and I did some prep work at one of them before moving on to work at a few dry cleaners. Eventually, David was hired at the Walmart Distribution Center. Not long after, he became seriously ill with congestive heart failure, and we began traveling back and forth to Richmond for his treatments.

The children were facing challenges in school, and we did our best to support them through it.

Then came an unexpected call; we were asked to pick up our godson in Emporia. He was just a newborn, and his mother had to go to jail. We weren't prepared for this, not emotionally or logistically, but we stepped in and got everything ready to care for him.

Around that time, I started working night shifts at Ingram Books to help support our growing household.

In 1998, I discovered a lump in my breast and underwent a biopsy. The diagnosis was breast cancer. I had a modified radical mastectomy, but did not receive radiation or chemotherapy. Instead, I was prescribed Tamoxifen.

David encouraged me to stop taking the medication, and I chose to trust God for my healing.

Praise God, praise God—You are so good!

Psalm 145:3–5: *"Great is the Lord, and greatly to be praised; and his greatness is unsearchable. One generation shall praise thy works to another, and shall declare thy mighty acts. I will speak of the glorious honor of thy majesty, and of thy wondrous works."*

I almost forgot this part of the story. One night, David walked out of the trailer to leave for work. Moments later, he ran back inside, barely able to speak.

"Call 911!" he gasped. "There's a car coming—airborne. If it hits the pole about 100 to 200 feet from us, or if it hits the trailer—we're all dead."

It was a terrifying moment. We didn't know what would happen next, but God protected us.

Psalm 28:7: *"The Lord is my strength and my shield, my heart trusts in him, and he helps me. My heart leaps for joy, and with my song I praise Him."*

We all have a story to tell, so don't be afraid to share yours. I remember a pastor once told me, *"Tell the people—run and tell that!"*

1 Thessalonians 5:18: *"In everything give thanks; for this is the will of God in Christ Jesus concerning you."*

I'm sure Pastor G. Lee and the members of Scott Zion remember the day David walked into church just fine, but left in an ambulance headed to the hospital. It was a frightening moment, one of many.

But God is so faithful. *He was there all the time.* Through it all—every trial, every tear—*He was there all the time.*

God has opened many doors, and closed some too. But He has always been by my side, walking with me through countless tests and challenges.

"I can't go back. I won't go back." Trust God and see what He'll do. Sometimes, He sends someone to a service you're attending, and in that moment, you both begin to cry and forgive each other—for things said, for misunderstandings, for wounds that needed healing.

Thank you, Jesus! Thank you, Jesus!

We may have lost some battles, but God won the wars.

We cared for our godson for about a year or two and tried to get help for him, but resources were limited. After much prayer, we felt it was best for him to be with his brother and family in Illinois. We contacted his aunt, and she came to pick him up.

Financially, things were tight. All we had coming in was David's unemployment and my income from work. Bills were piling up, and we were on the verge of eviction.

God is an on-time God. Just when we were about to lose everything, David's disability came through, and we were able to pay our bills. The church we were attending initially refused to help, but eventually, they did. *Won't He do it?*

In 2000, we returned home to Lynchburg, but the house wasn't ready. Looking back, I realize those two situations were lessons in patience. While waiting for the house to be finished, we stayed with David's cousin down the street. After dinner one evening, I took a nap, grateful for a moment of rest.

Our son had completed Job Corps and was living independently in Hopewell. Our daughter and her family had their own place in Petersburg. We prayed for them to move to Lynchburg, and God answered that prayer. *Amen!* They stayed with us for a while before moving into the apartment below ours.

Philippians 4:12: "*I know how to be abased, and I know how to abound: in everything and in all things have I learned the secret both to be filled and to be hungry, both to be abound and to suffer need.*"

Philippians 4:13: "*I can do all things in him that strengthened me.*"

Yes, we had two vehicles repossessed.

Hebrews 13:5: "*Let your conversations be without covetousness; and be content with such things as ye have; for he hath said, I will never leave thee, nor forsake thee.*"

CHAPTER 4

Say No to You, You, and You

I used to think my husband struggled with saying no, but now I realize, I do too. I've had to learn to shut off the television, silence the phone, and eliminate distractions. It's not easy, but it's necessary.

Saying no is like stopping a child from touching a hot stove or running into the street after a ball; it's protective, not punitive. In my own life, I've made too many excuses and allowed too many interruptions. I've had to face the truth: I must learn to say no—to you, you, and you.

Have you ever wanted something so deeply, but God said no? Or felt the urge to speak your mind to someone, but the Spirit held you back?

In order to complete this project, I've had to say no to you, you, and you.

Is it hard to say no? Yes, it is. But it's part of the process.

Life is a journey, isn't it?

It's a rollercoaster of ups and downs, twists, turns, and unexpected stops. But every part of it teaches us something.

CHAPTER 5

History

David once told me that the first time he saw me was at Jefferson Forest High School, during an event hosted by DECA (Distributive Education Clubs of America). DECA is an organization that prepares young leaders and entrepreneurs for careers in marketing, finance, hospitality, and management.

He said he told his friends right then, *"That's going to be my wife."* His mother, Ma Cora, shared that he would even call my name in his sleep. She used to say she'd be so glad when he finally found Barbara.

And speaking of Ma Cora, she made the best strawberry cakes. *Yum, yum, yum!*

Some of my favorite hobbies include writing, reading, fishing, watching the Olympics, and listening to music. Before we moved in May of 1993, I graduated as a certified nursing assistant (CNA) through career training. In October 1997, I received my missionary license. I answered my call to preach and was officially licensed in April 2002.

In 2001, we founded Divine Love Revival Center, and later, in September 2015, we established Trust in God Ministry. Over the years, I held many private duty jobs caring for the elderly, a role I truly loved. Seniors are so much fun, almost like children, and they carry so much wisdom. I remember one lady I cared for who didn't like to take baths. I had to get creative to convince her, and though she often complained about being cold, she loved when I applied lotion to her skin. She once told me I should become a masseuse! I was also known for being a driven and dedicated hostess.

After we moved back to Lynchburg, David began dialysis treatments. At first, he went to the center, but eventually we were able to train for home dialysis. This was a much better option; it allowed the machine to run for eight hours at a slower pace, rather than the rapid three to four hours at the center that left him completely exhausted.

I'll never forget the days when the nurse would blow the horn before even reaching the house because David was having a seizure. She would help me get him inside and lay him down. Those were hard, frightening days.

Thankfully, we were able to get some help with light housework and meal preparation since I was working outside the home. Still, it was frustrating to learn that I, as his wife, couldn't be paid to care for him, while others who didn't know him as well could. Eventually, our daughter stepped in and said, "Let me check into taking care of my daddy." And she was more than glad to do it.

It was exhausting at times, working from 9:00 a.m. to 5:00 or 6:00 p.m., then coming home to set David up on the dialysis machine. It was hard, but God gave me the strength to keep going.

Thankfully, we were able to travel with the machine. Most of the supplies could be shipped to wherever we were staying. Our first vacation with the children and our godson was to Williamsburg; it was beautiful there. I also remember the last trip David drove to: Baltimore, Maryland. Grandson, he and I went together. It was incredible to see him drive that far, and we had a wonderful time.

David was on dialysis for eighteen years, a remarkable span, especially considering how many people he dialyzed with didn't make it that long. The first church we joined as a family was Mt. Shiloh Baptist Church in Monroe, Virginia, along with his mother.

David and I were married for forty-two years, and it was good. There was so much I didn't know at the beginning, but over time, I learned, and the first lesson was communication. *Yes, communication.* I'm sure we both learned a lot from each other.

Life must be balanced. *Love the Lord, seek Him first, and serve Him.* And don't forget to have a hobby, something that brings you joy. What do you love to do?

If you weren't loved as a child or told you were loved, do you truly know what love is, or how to give it? My parents weren't there for me, but *thank God, He was!*

I thank God for all the people in my life. *You are not in my life by accident, and I love you.* These experiences have shaped my character, molded my personality, and humbled me.

David was already facing health challenges when I met him. He would black out from bleeding ulcers, and his blood pressure was never stable. Over time, his condition worsened; he developed congestive heart failure, kidney failure, and diabetes, and had to undergo procedures to place stents in his heart.

Through it all, we lived out the vows we made: "For better, for worse, for richer, for poorer, in sickness and in health, to love and to cherish, until death do us part."

CHAPTER 6

Goin' Fishing

Ma Mabel and I shared a special love for fishing. We had two or three favorite spots in Boonsboro. She would settle on one side of the lake, and I'd be on the other, cheering loudly every time I caught something. I even caught a turtle once! I remember leaving my fish on a chain in the water, and one day when I pulled the line up, something had eaten half of them.

A few years ago, I revisited one of those lakes; it was still there, just as I remembered. I had learned how to dig for worms, bait the hook, reel in the fish, and even clean them. Fishing became an experience I truly enjoyed, though I haven't gone since Ma Mabel passed. I did get my license and hope to go again soon, before it expires. Back then, we didn't need a license. Fishing is a quiet, calming sport—no talking, just peace. It's one of the most refreshing things I've ever known.

To My Beloved Husband: Apostle David

First, I want to say, I miss you deeply and love you dearly. I'm so grateful we had forty-two years together and were married three times to each other. There were moments of misunderstanding, but we made it through. I wish you were here to read my book and poems. I thought they were lost forever after falling into the wrong hands, but God had a sweeter plan.

I still can't believe you drove all the way to Baltimore, Maryland. That trip was unforgettable. I'm so glad Kymari went with us, pushing that wheelchair was no small task. I can hardly write this through the tears.

You were deeply rooted in the Word of God. Your impersonation of Mr. Brown was spot-on, and your resemblance to Bishop T.D. Jakes always amazed me. We shared many beautiful memories, and some painful ones too. It was especially hard seeing you at UVA after your final back surgery. But through it all, I thank God He didn't let you suffer.

To My Son Azell:

Don't Quit

Do you remember I once gave you a poem entitled "Don't Quit"

> When things go wrong as they sometimes will
> When the road you're trudging seems all up hill
> When the funds all low and the debts are high
> And you want to smile, but you have to sigh
> When your care is pressing you down a bit
> Rest if you must, but don't you quit
>
> Life is strange with its twists and turns
> As everyone of us sometimes learns
> And many a fellow comes about
> When he might have won had he stuck it out
> Don't give up though the pace seems slow
> You may succeed with another blow
>
> Success is failure turned inside out
> The silver tint of the clouds of doubt
> And you never can tell just how close you are
> It may be near when it seems afar
> So, stick to the fight when you're hardest hit
> It's when things seem worst that you must not quit

For all the sad words of tongue or pen

The saddest are these:

> "It Might Have Been"
> By John. G. Whittier
> 1807–1892

Remember Philippians 4:6–7: "*Be careful for nothing; but in everything by prayer and supplication with thanksgiving let your request be made known onto God. And the peace of God passes all understanding, shall keep your hearts and minds through Christ Jesus.*"

I love you, Azell!

I'm so grateful you're home and no longer homeless in Texas. The Scott Zion family prayed for you, wherever you were, and I'm so thankful we can talk now.

Please use the gifts God has given you. Dream. Inspire. Create. Imagine. Hope. Believe. Trust. Love. And have faith.

Thank you and DeeDee for blessing us with my handsome grandson, Kaleb.

Deuteronomy 31:8: "*And the Lord he it is that doth go before thee, neither forsake thee, fear not, neither be dismayed.*"

To My Daughter Tee:

I'm so grateful that you and Daddy were able to spend time together. We prayed earnestly for you to come home, and God answered that prayer.

Dream. Imagine. Create. Inspire. Hope. Believe. Trust. Love. And above all, have faith.

Remember Philippians 4:6–7: "*Be careful for nothing; but in everything by prayer and supplication with thanksgiving let your request be made known onto God. And the peace of God passes all understanding, shall keep your hearts and minds through Christ Jesus.*"

God answers *knee-mail*.

Never give the devil a ride—he'll always want to drive.

Can't sleep? Try counting your blessings.

Forbidden fruit creates many jams.

Christians, keep the faith, but don't keep it from others.

Satan subtracts and divides. God multiplies.

If you don't want to reap the fruits of sin, stay out of the devil's orchard.

Look forward, not behind.
—*DLRC (Divine Love Revival Center) Newsletter*

Deuteronomy 31:8: "*And the Lord, he it is that doth go before thee; he will be with thee, he will not fail thee, neither forsake thee: fear not, neither be dismayed.*"

Thank you and Corey for my beautiful grandbabies.

To My Son Desmond:

I'm so sorry you lost your mother. I know you found your father and met him, but didn't get the chance to spend much time together. I want you to know: I love you deeply.

Remember Deuteronomy 31:8: "*And the Lord, he it is that doth go before thee, neither forsake thee, fear not, neither be dismayed.*"

To My Grandchildren:

Miah – The Organizer
Lisha – Detective Gadget
Ky-mari – Mr. Tech
Kaleb – KB
Alaysia – Little Bunny
Zara – Firecracker
Kymarion – Little Man

It's been a joy to watch you all grow up and spend time with you. In humility, value others above yourselves not looking to your own interests.

Ecclesiastes 3:8: *"A time to love, a time to hate; a time to war, and a time for peace."*

Philippians 2:1–4: *"If there be therefore any consolation in Christ if any comfort of love, if any fellowship of the spirit, if any bowels and mercies. Fulfilled ye my joy, that you be like minded, having the same love, being of one accord, of one mind. Let nothing be done through strife or vain glory; but in loneliness of mind that each esteem other better than themselves. Look not in everyman on his own things, but everyman also on the things of others."*

God loves you, and Nana B. does too.

Don't ever forget the memories of Papa David!

To My Grandchildren to Come:

Nana B. loves you!

Some may ask, *Why poems?*

I write poems because they connect me to God in a way that feels timeless. Even before I fully knew Him, I believe He was speaking to me through poetry. His promise to give me an expected end, and His assurance that He knew me before my parents did, is being revealed through every verse.

Others may wonder, *What is it about poems in particular?*

Poems are often short and to the point, yet full of meaning. They make me pause, reflect, and experience a "Selah" moment. I've always been someone who likes to get to the heart of things, but I also want what I say to carry weight. Tell me what you're thinking, what you want, and let's get to it.

God Himself spoke in parables and poetic language. He invites us to pause and review. The peace I feel when writing poetry is indescribable. I wanted to share that peace with my children, and with their children, and generations to come.

We all face seasons of war and long for peace. Peace is our preference, but it often comes through challenge, crisis, and conflict, whether within ourselves, with others, or with the questions we carry. God reassures us, sometimes in the smallest paragraphs of a poem.

Each scripture I've included is meant to encourage, enlighten, and equip you in some way. Take time to discover your purpose—your reason for being.

Remember, we all have a purpose, and it often shows up in the form of a project. That project may come during a season when you feel overwhelmed or too busy. But that's exactly when you'll need to say, *"I have a project of my own."*

It's tied to your purpose and to the plan that God Himself has for your life.

Please remember: when building a project, nothing comes already assembled. There must be development, repair, and intentional effort to bring it together.

Poems are just one part of me. I'm not naturally an extrovert; I'm more of an introvert. I think of the biblical figure Joseph, often called "the silent man." He was underrated, frequently misunderstood, but he was the *faithful guardian of our Redeemer*.

This has been the story of my life. Only now do I fully realize: *I have been the project.* I've been fulfilling God's purpose, working on myself, piece by piece.

Stand Up

Stand right up and save your soul

It's something you must do

Stand right up and save your soul

It's all left up to you

Stand right up and save your soul

Don't waste too much time

So stand right up and save you soul

And clean your troubled mind

You know, brother and sister, we got

To mean it from the heart

We all got to make that journey

So you might as well make a start

So get on up, my brother and sister

and let the journey begin

Give God your hand and He

Will take away your sins

Get on up and save your soul

That's something you got to do

Get on up and save your soul

Nobody can do it but you

Get on up and let go of your

sin and feel good within

And when they open up the

Big white gates you can

Walk right on in.

By William Oliver

❀ ❀ ❀ ❀ ❀

Mother's

What kind of mother would I be
If Jesus hadn't stopped to rescue me
He came in to my heart
To give me a brand-new start

With heartache, pain, misery, and strife
I'm so glad Jesus is in my life
He told me what love really means
He's the best teacher I've ever seen

A mother shouldn't be controlling and demanding but full of
Love and understanding
A mother should be concerned about their children playing
In the street and running wild

He continues to be a friend like no other
Jesus even taught me when I had no mother
For all you mothers who haven't come in
Give Jesus your hand and release your sins.

Pastor

Pastor, Pastor, without you the world would be a disaster

He's always on the go

But the family's moving so slow

Lots to do, people to see

But when the day is through

Thank you for all you do

God sent and true

Thank you for being a friend

And being there through thick and thin

Preaching, praying, and fasting

Teaching about a love that's everlasting

And preach the word in season and out

When they don't want to hear it

And don't want to shout.

Hello, Friends

I just like to say

It's great to see you here today, I'm glad you made it

And I wouldn't dare trade it, I love you

I appreciate you

And thanks so much.

Please, please stay in touch

Stay in God's will

Walk in God's way

Fast and pray, pray, pray.

My Husband

I love you, my dear

No matter how far or how near

I love you today, tomorrow, forever

In the mall, on the bus, or at the store

I'm glad God sent you my way and

You're always there on a rainy day

They said we wouldn't make it

God knows we sure couldn't fake it.

You Are Not Alone

You are not alone

Because God is on the throne

He sees your tears

And calms your fears

He is there to lead and guide you

To protect you

He'll never forget you

He'll never neglect you

You are not alone.

Spring

Spring, Spring

It's time to do your thing

Isn't it beautiful

To see the dawning of a new day

The sunrise and blue skies

Isn't it amazing

And worth gazing

God made a wonderful creation

Look at the trees trying to bloom

It will be time to plant soon

A lot more daytime

Means more playtime.

My Cat

I have this sweet, adorable cat

He loves me no matter where I am at

He sleeps in my bed

Not at my foot but at my head

He likes to eat

Anything long as it's meat.

Let Go, Let God

If you let go and let God

You would really be amazed

You could break out with a praise

Sing a song or maybe throw in a dance

Because it will help you with your circumstance

Clap your hands or run around

They might tell you look like a clown

But nobody knows like you

Everything God brought you through

Tell your neighbor, excuse me

But I got to thank him, you see

You don't know like I know this ain't no show

You can't tell it, let me tell it.

To Appreciate

What does appreciation mean?

To be grateful, thankful for something unseen

Whether big or small

Whenever you answer the call

We appreciate you

And everything you do

So Happy Appreciation Day

We all love you in a different way.

Who Did It

Who made the highest mountain

Who made the water fountain

And even the deep blue seas

Who made the heavenly skies

And the birds that fly so high

Who made the leaves to blow

And the clouds to move graceful and slow

All creatures big and small

Yes, God made them one and all.

Who Is This Man?

Do you know the man Jesus Christ?

Do you know the man Jesus Christ?

Has He done anything in your life?

He died on the cross

So your soul wouldn't be lost

His Blood was shed for you and me

As they marched Him up Calvary

He heals, delivers, and sets us free

Without Him, where would we be?

He wipes every tear from your eye

Yet you won't serve Him, Oh why!

He was beaten beyond recognition

For a very important mission

That our souls might never die.

A Good Neighbor

Who could ask for a better neighbor

Who is willing to do any favor

It's good to have a friend

Not in everybody you can depend

She's very concerned and in the word she is learned

As I end this letter, who can ask for a anything better

One who cares

And a meal she will share.

Father's Day

A Dad is a person who is loving and kind,

And often he knows what you have on your mind.

He's someone who listens, suggests, and defends.

A Dad can be one of your very best friends!

He's proud of your triumphs,

But when things go wrong,

A Dad can be patient, helpful, and strong

In all that you do, a Dad's love plays a part.

There's always a place for you in his heart.

And each year that passes, you're even more glad,

More grateful and proud just to call him Dad!

Thank you, Dad . . .

For listening and caring, for giving and sharing,

But especially for just being you.

Happy Father's Day!

Relaxing

Alone, just Jesus and I

Peace, quiet, and tranquility

Listening for the sound of his voice

Because there isn't a better choice

Taking my mind off myself, self, self . . .

Sitting under the moonlight

Into the dark sacred night

Watching the leaves fall from the trees

Close your eyes and feel the breeze

Oh, what a wonder, just to watch the sea.

Lord, I Love You

Lord, I love you in so many ways

I couldn't tell you all in a day

You woke me up one more time

In my right mind

What a beautiful sunrise!

You let me see from my own eyes

Jesus, I love you

Because of all you do

Every breath I take comes from you

You wipe away every tear

And take away all my fears.

Mother

You gave us life one summer and winter day

I couldn't tell you all in a day

You cared for us in your own gentle way

You taught us all from

A to Z

With the help of God, you raised and believed in me

You said we were special, one of a kind

My brother and I

We seldom said "thank you" but you didn't mind

Some kids aren't fortunate to have a loving mother but

I thank God for you and Dad too!

You've been there my whole life through

So in my own way

I'm saying

Thank you

Hugs and kisses

Tee

and

Azell

Ma Katie

To a special lady

Her name is Ma Katie

What can I say

My sister, My friend

Through thick and thin

You took me in

You cared, You loved, and shared

I could call you on the phone

When I felt all alone

When friends left and turned their backs

To you I could always chat

So just remember it's your time

Don't you see all the signs

This is your day

And we come to celebrate it

In a special way

Jennifer

You were one of a kind aide, and by our side you stayed

A dear and true friend

And we loved you until the end

We lost touch for sometime

But you were always on our mind

Jenn, Jenn

Where have you been

I was so glad when you called

Whether it was summer or fall

Together or a part

You'll always be in my heart.

As the movie *The Ribbon* beautifully reminds us,
"Take the ingredients of your life and make something out of it."

www.ingramcontent.com/pod-product-compliance
Lightning Source LLC
Chambersburg PA
CBHW030222140626
46545CB00012B/2852